NoLex 12/12

Famous Explorers

Samuel de Champlain

Claude Hurwicz

The Rosen Publishing Group's
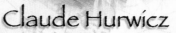
PowerKids Press™
New York

To Amy Hurwicz and Gregory Hurwicz

Published in 2001 by The Rosen Publishing Group, Inc.
29 East 21st Street, New York, NY 10010

Photo Credits: Cover photo, pp. 1, 2, 3, 7, 12, 20 © The Granger Collection; p. 2 © Art Resource; pp. 4, 8, 11 © CORBIS/BETTMANN; p. 15 © CORBIS; p. 16 © North Wind Pictures; p. 19 © WARD, BALDWIN/CORBIS-BETTMANN.

First Edition

Book Design: Maria E. Melendez and Felicity Erwin

Hurwicz, Claude.
     Samuel de Champlain / Claude Hurwicz.— 1st ed.
        p. cm.— (Famous explorers. Set 2)
     Includes index.
     Summary: A biography of the French explorer who founded Quebec, discovered Lake Champlain, and was called the Father of New France.
     ISBN: 0-8239-5559-1 (alk. paper)
     1. Champlain, Samuel de, 1567–1635—Juvenile literature. 2. Explorers—America—Biography—Juvenile literature. 3. Explorers—France—Biography—Juvenile literature. 4. New France—Discovery and exploration—French—Juvenile literature. 5. America—Discovery and exploration—French—Juvenile literature. [1. Champlain, Samuel de, 1567–1635. 2. Explorers. 3. New France—Discovery and exploration.] I. Title. II. Series.

F1030.1.C495 H86 2000
971.01'13'092—dc21
[B]   00-023931

Manufactured in the United States of America

Contents

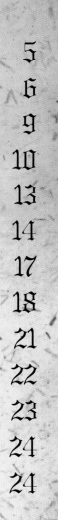

The Father of New France

amuel de Champlain was born in 1567 in Brouage, a seaside town in France. Little is known about Champlain's childhood, except that he loved the sea and liked to draw. Both his father and uncle were sea captains. This led Champlain to become an **explorer**, **navigator**, and mapmaker. Champlain is best known as the Father of New France. New France is now part of Canada. In the early 1600s, Champlain guided many French settlers to start a new life there.

Samuel de Champlain loved the sea. He also liked to draw. He grew up to become an explorer and mapmaker.

Life As a Soldier

When Champlain was a young man, a war was being fought in France. The **Huguenots**, today called Protestants, and the Catholics were fighting each other. Champlain fought on the side of the Catholics. He fought under the **command** of Henry of Navarre. In 1589, Henry of Navarre became King Henry IV of France. As a soldier, Champlain learned a great deal about **survival**. These survival skills would be useful when he became an explorer.

In 1598, Champlain was ready to take his first **voyage**. He signed up on a French ship that was going to Spain.

Henry of Navarre became king of France in 1589 after leading troops in the religious wars.

Gravé par B. Roger.

7

Early Travels

Champlain sailed to Spain with his uncle on a ship called the *Saint Julien*. In 1598, the *Saint Julien* was chosen to sail to Spanish lands in the Americas. These lands included what we now call Puerto Rico, Mexico, and Panama. Champlain traveled on the *Saint Julien* for almost three years. He wrote about all his experiences on this voyage. He also drew pictures and made maps of what he saw. When he got back to France, Champlain showed the maps to King Henry IV. The king was pleased with the work that Champlain had done. He thought the maps would help France learn more about the Americas. King Henry IV was so happy with Champlain that he gave him a title of **nobility**.

When he returned to France, Champlain showed King Henry IV his maps of the Americas.

The First Colony in Canada

King Henry IV of France sent Champlain on a trip to explore Canada. Champlain left France with three ships on March 15, 1603. When Champlain returned to France from his voyage, the king decided to send more people to Canada to start a **colony**. In 1604, Champlain traveled back to Canada to help start this colony.

Champlain and his men settled on Dochet Island (now called Saint Croix Island) in the Saint Croix River. This island is just off the coast of an area that used to be known as Acadia. Today this land is part of eastern Canada.

Saint Croix Island turned out to be a bad place for a colony. It was hard for the **colonists** to grow food. The winter there was very cold. Many colonists died of a disease called **scurvy**.

Champlain set up his colony on what is now Saint Croix Island. This island is off the coast of what used to be called Acadia. This map shows Acadia in 1755.

ACADIA,
WITH
ADJACENT ISLANDS.
1755.

11

Neuville.

Cul de Sac

Beau Po

12

Quebec

After failing to **colonize** Dochet Island, Champlain and his men spent two years at another place in Acadia called the Annapolis Basin. During that time, Champlain reached a place on the Saint Lawrence River called Quebec. The Native Americans already living there had given it that name. Champlain returned to France and got permission from King Henry IV to start a French colony in Quebec.

On July 3, 1608, Champlain and 28 colonists started building a shelter. Soon the weather turned cold. Food was hard to find. Only Champlain and eight colonists survived the winter. From this hard beginning, the colony of Quebec began to grow. Today Quebec is still the center of French-speaking Canada.

Champlain started a colony in Quebec. This picture shows Quebec in 1758, 150 years after the French colonists arrived there.

13

Champlain and the Native Americans

Champlain became friends with two Native American groups in Canada. These groups were the Algonquins and the Hurons. They promised to help Champlain with the fur trade. The fur trade was an important way for the French colonists to make money. The Native Americans knew the land well. They offered to guide Champlain through different parts of Canada. They wanted Champlain's help in return. The Algonquins and Hurons wanted him to fight against their enemy, the Iroquois. Champlain agreed to help the Algonquins and the Hurons fight the Iroquois. The **partnership** between the French and these Native American groups lasted for more than a hundred years.

Native Americans helped guide Champlain as he explored Canada. ➤

Lake Champlain and the Iroquois

In 1609, Champlain made his first trip **inland** from the Saint Lawrence River. Guided by the Native Americans, Champlain went south into the lands of the Iroquois. Then he traveled on what is now the Richelieu River. There he found a huge and beautiful lake. He named it Lake Champlain.

At the lake, Champlain and the Hurons ran into their enemy, the Iroquois. Champlain used a gun called a **musket** during a battle against the Iroquois. The Native Americans didn't fight with guns. They fought with bows and arrows. Champlain and the Hurons won the battle. The Algonquins and the Hurons admired Champlain's power and strength. He had earned their respect.

Champlain used a musket to fight the Iroquois.

Exploring Canada

Champlain's life in Canada was full of adventure. In 1610, he won another battle against the Iroquois.

Champlain continued to explore Canada. He took a Native American boat called a **canoe** through very dangerous waters. These waters were called the Lachine Rapids. These rapids are just north of what is now the city of Montreal. Champlain was one of the first Europeans to go through these rapids.

In 1613, Champlain went up the Ottawa River by canoe. He wanted to help the French strengthen the fur trade. He was looking for new areas to find animals for fur. It was a difficult journey. He made maps of all the new places he saw as he traveled.

Champlain used a canoe to explore different parts of Canada.

The Great Lakes

In 1615, the Algonquins and the Hurons asked Champlain to help them fight the Iroquois again. The Native Americans and Champlain agreed to meet in the land of the Hurons. Then they would leave to fight the Iroquois. When they met on the shores of Lake Huron, Champlain saw the lakes now known as the Great Lakes for the first time. The Great Lakes are huge bodies of water between the countries of Canada and the United States.

The war party crossed the Great Lakes and arrived in what is now called New York State. Champlain was hurt by an arrow during the battle with the Iroquois. He was carried back to the shores of Lake Huron. Champlain had lost this battle. Still, he had explored more new **territory** and had seen the Great Lakes.

Champlain crossed the Great Lakes, shown in this map, to help the Algonquin and Huron Indians fight the Iroquois.

Champlain's Final Years

In his final years, Champlain helped the colony of Quebec grow. He also wrote books about his adventures. In 1628, France and England were at war. The English captured Quebec. They took Champlain as a prisoner. When the war ended, Champlain was released. In 1632, England gave Quebec back to France. Champlain returned to Quebec. He died there in 1635. For all of his discoveries, Champlain will be remembered as the Father of New France.

Samuel de Champlain's Timeline

1567-Champlain is born in a seaside town in France.

1603-Champlain sails to Canada for the first time.

1608-Champlain and his men begin a colony in Quebec.

1635-Champlain dies in Quebec on Christmas day.

Glossary

canoe (kuh-NOO) A light, narrow boat with pointed ends that is moved through the water by paddling.

colonists (KAH-luh-nists) People who live in a colony.

colonize (KAHL-uh-nyz) To settle in a new land and claim it for the government of another country.

colony (KAH-luh-nee) An area in a new country where a large group of people move, who are still ruled by the leaders and laws of their old country.

command (kuh-MAND) The leadership of others.

explorer (ik-SPLOR-er) A person who travels to different places to learn more about them.

Huguenots (YOO-gan-ots) A religious group of people living in France during the 1500s. They later became known as Protestants.

inland (IN-lind) Land that is not near the water.

musket (MUS-kit) A big, long gun used by soldiers before the invention of the rifle.

navigator (NA-vuh-gay-tur) An explorer of the seas.

nobility (noh-BIL-ih-tee) Members of royalty or other high-ranking people in a kingdom.

partnership (PART-ner-ship) When two or more people join together for a specific cause.

scurvy (SKUR-vee) A disease in which a person's teeth fall out from lack of fruits and vegetables.

survival (sur-VYV-al) Staying alive.

territory (TEHR-uh-tohr-ee) Land that is controlled by a person or group of people.

voyage (VOY-ij) A trip taken by water.

Index

Web Sites

To learn more about Samuel de Champlain, check out these Web sites:

http://www.samueldechamplain.com/

http://www.encyclopedia.com/articles/02533.html